4

811.5
Williams, Tennessee

Androgyne, mon
amour

DATE DUE

RENEWABLE   4

Androgyne, Mon Amour

Androgyne, Mon Amour

Poems by

Tennessee Williams

A NEW DIRECTIONS BOOK

Grateful acknowledgment is made to the editors and publishers of books and magazines in which some of the poems in this volume first appeared: *Ambit, Evergreen Review, Five Young American Poets* (Third Series, 1944), *New Directions in Prose and Poetry,* and *Prairie Schooner.* "Tangier: The Speechless Summer" and "Miss Puma, Miss Who?" were originally published in *Antaeus.* "Crepe-de-chine" first appeared in the *New Yorker.*

Manufactured in the United States of America
First published clothbound in 1977
Published simultaneously in Canada by McClelland & Stewart, Ltd.

Library of Congress Cataloging in Publication Data

Williams, Tennessee, 1911–
    Androgyne, mon amour,
    (A New Directions Book)
    I. Title.
PS3545.I5365A68   811'.5'4   76–52956
ISBN 0–8112–0648–3

New Directions Books are published for James Laughlin
by New Directions Publishing Corporation,
333 Sixth Avenue, New York 10014

The Contents

Androgyne, Mon Amour

OLD MEN GO MAD AT NIGHT

I

Old men go mad at night
but are not Lears

There is no kingly howling of their rage,
their grief, their fears, dementedly,
from sea-cliff into storm.

What's left
is keeping hold of breath
and for cover never now a lover
rests them warm.

No title of dignity, now,
no height of old estate

Gives stature to the drama . . .

Ungrateful heirs, indeed!
Their treacherous seed

Turns them away from more than tall
gold-hammered doors:

Exiles them into such enormous night
skies have no room for it

And old men have no Fools except themselves.

II

Why is so much still wanted
in such a small place, haunted
by such —

No, pain's not much.
Premonitory twinges . . .

Oh, later, greater
but by then too late:

Pain's courier
throws into panic of flight
before

Banner and drums and all of
armored might . . .

There is a wink of light
above a bedroom sill
until —

Was that a board that creaked
as he took leave of us,
or did he speak —
"I'm going to sleep, good night . . . "

I have used the earth, I have abused the earth
Now must I lose the earth.

No breath for such a cry,
if there were thought or tongue . . .

Old men were never young.

"WINTER SMOKE IS BLUE AND BITTER"

Winter smoke is blue and bitter:
women comfort you in winter.

Scent of thyme is cool and tender:
girls are music to remember.

Men are made of rock and thunder:
threat of storm to labor under.

Cypress woods are demon-dark:
boys are fox-teeth in your heart.

DARK ARM, HANGING OVER THE EDGE OF INFINITY

I

Dark arm, hanging over the edge of infinity,
what have you let go of,
what are your fingers dangling emptily towards?

This is the moment of continued momentum
but will not continue forever.
The spheres will relax,
will suddenly drop out of heaven,
unless you resume your skillful manipulation.

Sleeping Negro, wake up,
bestir your dark copper limbs,
the rhythm is broken, there is danger in heaven!

II

Dark arm, hanging over the edge of infinity,
sleeping athlete,
fingers relaxed, grasping nothing,
what have you let go of?

Something must have become
of the luminous white plaything
that the fingers were made
for curving firmly around.

Dreaming ball-player,
drinker of the warm white milk of space,
prostrated Negro juggler,
skillful manipulator of a million glittering spheres,
Wake up, wake up!

Suspense is ended —
Heaven is full of the sound of shattering glass!

EVENTS PROCEED

Events proceed in different localities.
In Florence Visconti is producing *Troilus and Cressida*.
This is simultaneous with my agony in Rome.
But Visconti operates with his own system of co-ordinates
and I with mine, and the word simultaneous
has a doubtful meaning.

I am distressed by the fear of stammering when I speak.
Perhaps Visconti is distressed by the fear of failure to produce
a great spectacle.
                        Both of us fear people: I of speaking to people,
Visconti of what people will say.
           These fears are supposed to be co-existent in time.
Humility could be the cure of each. If I were humble enough
      to be unconcerned:
           if Visconti were humble enough to be unconcerned.
           But pride tortures both.

We are supposed to be co-existent in time.
           Events make time: when events are so different, how
can time be the same?

           When events are so. Time. System.
           The very words begin to drop out of their meanings.

      (Perhaps my life has done enough good when I open
the doors of a state asylum for my sister, if only for three days
a week, in a place called Lead Wood, Missouri.)

ANDROGYNE, MON AMOUR

I

Androgyne, mon amour,
brochette de coeur was plat du jour,
     (heart lifted on a metal skewer,
     encore saignante et palpitante)
where I dined au solitaire,
table intime, one rose vase,
     lighted dimly, wildly gay,
as, punctually, across the bay
mist advanced its pompe funèbre,
its coolly silvered drift of gray,
     nightly requiem performed for
mourners who have slipped away . . .

Well, that's it, the evening scene,
mon amour, Androgyne.

     Noontime youths,
thighs and groins tight-jean-displayed,
     loiter onto Union Square,
junkies flower-scattered there,
     lost in dream, torso-bare,
young as you, old as I, voicing soundlessly
a cry,
     oh, yes, among them
revolution bites its tongue beneath its fiery
     waiting stare,
indifferent to siren's wail,
ravishment endured in jail.

16

Bicentennial salute?
Youth made flesh of crouching brute.

(Dichotomy can I deny of pity in a lustful eye?)

II

Androgyne, mon amour,
shadows of you name a price
exorbitant for short lease.
What would you suggest I do,
wryly smile and turn away,
fox-teeth gnawing chest-bones through?

Even less would that be true
than, carnally, I was to you
many, many lives ago,
requiems of fallen snow.

And, frankly, well, they'd laugh at me,
thick of belly, thin of shank,
spectacle of long neglect,
tragedian to public mirth.

(Chekhov's *Mashas* all wore black
for a reason I suspect:
Pertinence? None at all —
yet something made me think of that.)

"Life!" the gob exclaimed to Crane,
"Oh, life's a geyser!"
　　　　Oui, d'accord —
from the rectum of the earth.

Bitter, that. Never mind.
Time's only challenger is time.

III

Androgyne, mon amour,
cold withdrawal is no cure
for addiction grown so deep.
Now, finally, at cock's crow,
released in custody of sleep,
dark annealment, time-worn stones
          far descending,
no light there, no sound there,
entering depths of thinning breath,
farther down more ancient stones,
halting not, drawn on until

          Ever treacherous, ever fair,
          at a table small and square,
not first light but last light shows
(meaning of the single rose
where I dined au solitaire,
sous l'ombre d'une jeunesse perdue?)

          A ghostly little customs-clerk
          ("Vos documents, Mesdames, Messieurs?")
          whose somehow tender mockery
contrives to make admittance here
          at this mineral frontier
a definition of the pure . . .

          Androgyne, mon amour.

San Francisco, 1976

18

SPEECH FROM THE STAIRS

O lonely man,
the long, long rope of blood,
the belly's rope that swung you from your mother,
that dark trapeze your flesh descended from
unwillingly and with too much travail,
has now at last been broken lastingly —

You must turn for parentage toward the void,
you must remember further back than flesh,
for your first mother was not warm with blood,
no, she was cold with rock and white with fire
and deathless in her long embrace with time!
Look back that way —
Is there another way for you to go?

YOUNG MEN WAKING AT DAYBREAK

Young men waking at daybreak may be frightened at being
        evicted so much too quickly
from their unremembered, sheltering dreams of a mother.
        Suddenly, then, they may sense
the true enormity of exposure to chance. The morning,
        just beginning,
is full of whispered demands which they suspect
      they can't meet.
And whom do they have to trust
                        (assuming, recklessly,
they're still able to trust)
          but someone (you)
whose name has been shuffled back into last night's
        confusion of many?
They glance down at you warily as you turn and sigh
in your sleep.
           They're envious of it, your sleep,
which still protects you from whispers that seem each instant
to grow more distinct.
           They sit up, gingerly,
on the edge of your bed, hunched and shivering as old men
on benches, coughing their cigarette coughs . . .

Question: If you weren't sleeping,
would you call them back into warm oblivion with you,
        or, if you woke at this moment,
might they not be to you as nameless as you are to them
        and even less to be trusted? Probably yes,
        suspicion being
among the heraldic devices on the shield of your heart
        the one that seems most indelible,
as if carved or burned there.

        what, then, is there for them to do
but sit up gingerly on the edge of your bed, squinting into
        the prison light morning has given?

Will it be better at ten than it is at seven?

        Another question whose answer,
                equivocal, waits
on the magisterial tick of a watch, of many, so many watches,
        And so, without their names spoken
        or their hunched bodies touched,
they descend again into the mystery of the bed,
having first closed the shutters to hold the day back
        a while longer.

APPARITION

He speaks to the sea
and to the sky
that heed him not
and he asks not why.
Of light the silver,
it holds him not
nor emerald telling
tongues of gold.
Of holding, the truth is
nothing holds.
He's cold but he never
says he's cold,
He's old but he never
says he's old.
And youth is apparent
on his face,
a conjurer's trick
or a wanderer's grace
and the air of the world
still bears him away.

Will he return?
Oh, that he may,
and you'll hear again
what he did not say.

COUNSEL

I

Ask at the door for the man whose name I gave you.
You will probably find him sitting behind a newspaper
under a skylight that translates all weathers and hours
       into late winter dusk.

      His contempt means nothing,
                      for satiety has made him a eunuch,
and the glance that he gives you will come from
      behind the glass
wall of a dirty aquarium.
      His wife is another strange fish, perpetually agitating
the grey straws of a broom among a circular litter that
      travels nowhere.
      I think I had better advise you not to allow this lady to
conduct you upstairs upon the false excuse that her husband
      is busy.
      Her hot mouth exhales the steaming damp of
          a necropolis,
      but what's more important is her legerdemain.
While one hand diverts you obscenely, its more practical sister
wanders rapidly in and out of your pockets . . .
      Tip her extravagantly,
             not to secure her good will, since she doesn't
                            have any,
but a thousand francs will immobilize her fingers . . .

Jacques will present you with a little gray napkin,
    freshly ironed but not laundered,
and a key that looks as if it belonged to a forbidden closet
    of Bluebeard.
        Those items are not important.
        The candle is!

II

The candle is.
Its fitful illumination will see you into the future,
        partially, not completely,
but moments pass that way, and existence is moments'
    passage . . .

The stairs are windy,
Even the trembling of the hand that holds it is sufficient
        to blow
the flame of the candle out,
        and one must consider, before it's too late to consider,

The phenomena of light, and the perishability of it.

The phenomena of dark are sensible to the insensible only.
The nonphenomena of a mineral existence have
        an opposite luster,
the sort that a coal-bin has where no light is admitted:
they have a contrary weight and magnitude without measure,
        which is
inimical to us.

        Call it, if you will, terra incognita —
        but don't explore it until the command is issued . . .

I take this liberty, though: to remind you once more
that by some accident which is bewildering to God

                     Our roots are lodged
in a barely visible crevice among those immensities of
     black stone
that groan like the sea with their own oppressive
     nonbeing, groan
like a woman too old and dry for child-bearing, yet
     swollen with
child by a man detestable to her, a child that is lifeless, a
fetus of stone that grows in a belly of stone, in a body of stone
that endures without will of endurance:
        the stone is more ponderous than the stone that bears it!
        But light again, yes, the candle,
        exults in its being . . .

        Curve about it your palm,
        and if there's a mirror,
where often there is, at a certain turn of the stairs,
          don't look!

Don't think of how your face has disappeared into its tissue
For reality is a question that nobody asks any more.

III

Now take your time about selecting the girl
since most disappointments come from choosing too quickly.

I would advise you to sit down and order some wine.
     It's bad and expensive, but you don't have to drink it,
and the time it allows for inspecting the girls is worth it.

If twelve are present, easily five will be dogs,
    and the light is tricky,
but feels are permissible if there's suspicion of padding.
    The eager beavers are almost always the dogs,
    that's something
to go by, and personally I always flash my pocket lamp
    on the ones
in the corners that don't seem to know how they got there,
    obscurity being, at times, the velvet box of a pearl . . .

    Jacques can be helpful, if he's inclined to be helpful,
and a thousand francs can produce that inclination far
    more speedily
than the honest look in your eyes.
    Mais soyez tranquille! Take your time!
    And then, when you're ready,
nod to the girl you've selected: slip out, and she'll follow.

    Caress her thighs as she guides you.
    Let her do the opening, that's her business,
but say that the number is lucky, even if it's thirteen,
    for superstition's a kind of Esperanto . . .

    Oh, yes, something else which I had almost forgotten!
    It is better not to turn the light on until you have
lowered the torn green blind,
    and even then it is sometimes better not to,
for the roses on the wallpaper cannot bear remembrance,
nor can that almost invariable lithograph
    of Hope blindfolded with hands on a
    broken-stringed lyre.

IV

Now I don't suppose, since we are men of the world,
that it will be necessary for me to advise you against
the errors of adolescence,
                            among which is, first,
a romantic pity of self
            which takes the form of crocodile weeping for others.

            Don't impose on your own credulity, baby!

            The obituary column is really only an infinite
                            number of
variations upon the theme of your own eventual demise,
            and that's exactly why you skip past it so briskly
            en route to reports upon more fashionable doings.

            So here's the answer to all her lamentations: *Ho-hum!*
            And *don't* attempt to explain your neurosis to her,
                            If you fall in default upon the demands
                                        of her flesh,
            the convex being always a form of compulsion,
            Don't blame the girl for it!
            (A nasty temper's a worse mistake than compassion.)
                            And you must remember that it is certainly
            not to
her personal advantage for any patron to leave her
            without satisfaction.

V

Now understand this!
>I'm not a shill or a pimp,
>I don't get a cut from the house.
You asked me where you could go, I gave you this address,
but I don't give a goddamn whether you go there or not.
All I'm doing's informing you of its existence.

>Is that understood?
>Okay!

Sometimes a rubber breaks or a place is raided, and
>the John that
you sent there holds you responsible for it,
>So finally what—Uh-huh. I know what you mean.
>It's always as if something hadn't quite happened
between us, but what can you do?
>What's true, what's false,
when the heart's an old fake of a Gypsy squinting at tea-leaves!

>We shake hands at parting,
the valedictory phrase is *Au Revoir*,
>but after my hand has left yours,
I place it tenderly back in my own dark pocket. . . .

ONE HAND IN SPACE

I sing of the prodigal race,
the earlier dying,
the witchlike girls on the brooms
of morning flying,

The boys with the startled eyes
and covert hunger,
I sing of these, of their brief
and luckless number.

My mise-en-scene is the world
within the world,
the greenest of all green leaves
at the center curled.

I do not forbear to call
on demons driven
from mortal belief by the bells
of a proper heaven.

I ferret among the used
and exhausted lot
for the longing not wanted because
it was haunted and hot,

I want no purpose to own me
but only to say
I found these secretly burning
along the way,

This girl who was lost but knew
more places than one,
this boy who was blind but grew
the interior sun,

This point, this moment, this passage
a nameless place,
but holding forever curved
one hand in space!

IMPRESSIONS THROUGH A
PENNSY WINDOW

1. *Going Home*

I knew more surely than the name of my train, *The Crescent*,
      that I was now deep in The South
when I was wakened this morning to see on a railroad siding
      as we pulled lingeringly out of a town with a
          Choctaw or Cherokee name
      an old red caboose
miniature cupola set like a coquettish bonnet on its
      low-peaked roof,
         a flirty bit of balcony on its tail,
         nothing appearing outmoded and retired,
not faded from red into dim, paint-peeling pink,

      But all freshly brilliant,
assertively, jauntily garish in the hot morning sun of Georgia
      seeming to call *Hurry back* in a Southern girl's
         honeyed drawl,

And I swear that for a moment and a half, with a pride
      that dismayed me,
         that shook me somewhere deep under the
         Mason-Dixon line
of my divided psyche,
      I sensed, I felt, nearly heard
the dreadful anachronism of The Rebel Yell!
      It made me wonder at blood . . .

2. *Rival Breathers*

How much vegetation there still is in The South,
      the earth is overwhelmed with it,
devouring much of what we've been told is much less oxygen
      than the earth's air should hold.

And yet, despite Messrs. Cronkite-and-Sevareid's proper
      concern with ecology,
      I can't help feeling favorably impressed,
not because God is the unisexual propagator of all these
      generations of trees
and presumably of every citizen of the rooted,
      green-leaved kingdom,

      It is, I think, only a moment of self-forgetful homage
to the licentious abandon and valor of all this vegetation,
      this flagrantly wanton display of woods in lustrous leaf
and weeds in vivid flower,
prevailing against the pests and the pesticides and
      the oxygen failing . . .

THE COUPLE

I

I saw them often when they drove to Lyons,
a ghostly pair perched on a wooden scaffold.
They had a buffeted look, a shocked expression,
as though a cyclone had passed over lately.
But in their faded blues they were terribly clean.
They were clean as well-fed people never are.
They told their hunger in this woeful neatness
as much as in the fact they picked for food
on Saturday nights behind The White Cafe,
where vacant lots and tumbled fences gave
their moon-blanched business to the public view.

But it is morning that I see them in,
their gradual wagon, flaked with old manure,
unpolished gold on withered apple green,
is creaking toward the meridian back of a mare
that profane humor named The Holy Ghost,
her hip-joints cranking loud as ungreased axles,
her head ducked in a boiling pot of flies —
insensible or stoic, her skeleton seemingly bound
in worn-out carpet, the musty sort you find
in some old Mississippi lawyer's office —
and yet intent on traveling as they — the couple!
Not like comets! — but going where they planned.

Nothing could stop them!
>   I have seen them in
a wind that lifted a wheel clean off the road,
or when the river lapped upon the road —

Vertiginous the noon could spring upon them
and they would creep right underneath his heel,
things too imponderable for him to crush —
and he, the first exhausted, let them go.

It's all so wide in the Delta, and so level!
The seasons could walk across it four-abreast!
and still avoid the hidden cypress knees —
It's summer gradually in this slow-poke country:
first dogwood showing dimly in the brake:
then shimmerings all over — insect wings —
It seemed an apparition when July,
looming behind them as the Delta does,
made quivering pools of blueness where they moved,
and roosters warned the day not to go on —
Not to go on, for cotton is volcanic
in subtle ways: a noiseless dynamite
until October says Enough's enough
and hauls the sulphur country under rain.

II

Indians have less fixity of expression.
I never heard her speak nor saw him smile,
and yet their looks were mobile to each other,
enough to save them the expense of words
which doubtless they hoarded as old tomato tins
that took the place of cups for morning coffee.

34

I've seen them halt and clamber from their scaffold
with almost panicky haste for nothing more
than El Dorado glints of something tin
or broken promises of snowy china
not quite obscured in less distinguished rubble.
And she, unearthing it with bleeding knuckles,
would hold it up for his slow approbation
or for the sun's more humorous appraisal —
so enriched the caravan pushed on . . .

A child I was, but their gallantry impressed me,
and I stepped back from the road to watch them pass,
a silhouette that did a steady jig
between me and the levee or the sun.
          The gulf wind smelled of loneliness those mornings
and I created comrades out of air!
          But something else there was — less well-defined —
a whim of sunlight or more occult sign —
for always the faded woman smiled at me,
without quite looking at me, only her eyes
would brush me with a distant sort of feather,
that felt as sleep feels when you're very tired.

                    •   •   •

What is tremendous in the two was love.
I knew it by the stillness when they passed,
as they will always pass me in the South.

              Not flesh stormed by pellagra
nor demagogues that pin the donkey's tail —
     lynch trees,
                    novels,
                         sentiments of jasmine —

They are the South my grandmother faced me in
unflinching when a tornado struck the house
or curtains breathed into the house at noon
a lint of cotton from a throbbing gin —

Old boards dove-jointed — love . . .

This tenderness of such a weathered kind
was in the imprecision of their mouths,
the something not intended in their eyes,
as much as in that quiet wherein they moved
along Front Street when they had hitched the mare . . .
They'd watch the windows longer than you'd wait
for chicken dinner where you sat inside —
Their eyes embarrassed you with their soft wonder,
following spoons of soup into your mouth.
And slowly, slowly she would glance at him
as if to ask him some enormous question
in deference to his wisdom — He, the man,
would slightly touch her elbow — They'd move on . . .

So by degrees,
              by feints and hesitations,
from *Flynn's Emporium* where the block began
          to the *Delta Brilliant's* hot and smashing finale!

III

Through popcorn grease the babbling silver poured.
Some night of bedlam in a haunted house!
          An owl flown under a tablecloth assumed
the windy, weird dimensions of a spook —

The funny black man jumped out of his shoes!
You saw them smoking and the black man gone —
And you, and you —
Could you keep in your chair?

Ha-ha! The casements of the chest unlatched,
that comic Valentine, your heart, — escapes!
It sprinkles salt upon the peacock's tail —
It is the shipwreck and the albatross.
the moon of fantasy, the kiss of pain,
the icy mountains—flame!

At five o'clock the silver matinee
lets you out weakly on the lemoned street —
Yes, in the interim it's paled a bit
as though the hectic cinema had drawn
blood from it, too—and left it faint as you . . .

·   ·   ·

So far away—God, yes, so terribly far!
The Sunflower river takes such afternoons
in its long obligation to the Gulf —
No wonder childhood turns the Gulf so blue!

But you —
were sometimes with no warning left alone,
— schoolrooms,
façades,
— a disappearing trick.

You speak your name: repeat it in slow marvel:
the shock of your identity hits you so —
        It clubs you! Knocks you senseless nearly!
        I am *I!*
        The most preposterous circumstance of all —
        Identities, moments, their shock,
time neatly files them away and the contents, indexed,
        are finally one gray —
        then night? Of course,
predictable as was the day. . . . .

        Are all clothes uniforms?
        All beings one?

        IV

Lightning caught in a bottle!
        How long do fireflies live? my sister inquired
                of me once.
        Well, let's see.
We covered the top of the bottle of captured fireflies
        with a lid of some kind,
a broken shingle or brick and forgot them till dusk fell again.
        And then,
remembering that prison for flickering things,
        ran round the house to the back steps under which
those tiny thieves of fire had been locked up and abandoned
for twelve hours and found
        all small giddy sparkles extinguished,
        and so learned death.

                    •   •   •

Briefly reported in the *Press-Scimitar:*
Wagon containing old couple struck
    by train, demolished,
but the horse
    had crossed
        the tracks
and apparently had stopped there, stopped, just stopped,
    refusing to continue, and apparently the couple
had fallen asleep or been unable to descend in time, and then
    I learned a second lesson, possibly bigger than death,
the huge existence of lies.

EVENING

       Evening is her name.
She is waiting for you at the breathless height of the stairs,
and to admit you she draws the door soundlessly open
before you've had time to remove the doorkey
       from your pocket.
She is not Oriental and yet she's acquired the graces of the
       Far East.
They go with the skin exposed by the whispering
       poppy kimono,
that artfully careless permission of a breast's ivory satin
to be glimpsed as she draws the door further open with
       flickering eyes
and cool smile, suggestive of, "Yes, your touch
       I'll know later."
Why does she lift a finger to her lips, always as if the room,
       spacious and cool,
contained a music which is too delicate for a word to intrude
       upon it
or audible footsteps to fall?
There is an unspoken admonition, "Shoes off
       at the door, please."
And other silent gestures.
                 She indicates all about her
those many little enchantments which make the room safe
       to enter.
And terror is suspended at the threshold . . .

      Les points de suspension: Evening's ways of saying
that what you're about to say does not need saying.

40

All day you've been gone, and what has she done
    in your absence?
A number of leisurely things, accomplished with
    a quiet grace.
She has bathed in cool, scented water and dusted herself with
    rice powder,
        prepared herself for your return as a jewel
            for a birthday
is enclosed in gift-wrapping.
        Marvelously the window seems enlarged
            to three times its true size
and you feel that, leaning out of it,
        she has inhaled
    the freshness of a great distance:
then turned from the window to release it into the room's
    atmosphere
a moment before your return.
        She has made fragrant tea.
It is in pale blue bowls set on saucers, with crescents of lemon
cut so thinly they'll float on the pale amber surface,
lighter than liquid, than anything but the beginning of dusk.

Oh, she has long known how you love to stretch out on the floor
with your head resting on her lap that's softer than
    a silk cushion!
        And what else has she done in your absence?
All of the heavy furniture which offended you
    has been removed
        from the room, on the wide bed she has spread
fresh linen's landscape of snow.

Another mysterious marvel: she has widened
the table beside the bed to accommodate Rilke's stone angels
and the daring aerial leap and outcry of Crane
over Brooklyn's bridge and shipyards.

It is Evening's room prepared for your return.

Yet something now draws you toward the mysteriously
enlarged window.
You look out.
You see five stories below the level which took your breath
an apparitional youth.
He is standing directly below you and looking up at you
as you look down at him.
Then all of Evening's enchantments are dissolved
in that luminous upward look, innocent, but an enticement.
And he is Evening, then, instead of she who was Evening
and descending the stairs takes your breath
more completely
than did ascending.
Is He there when you rush from the entrance?
Angelic, inquiring, inviting?
Not even the mist that seemed to envelop his gleam.
And what a long breathless climb back up the five flights to—
she is Evening again.
Again She receives you, a finger to her lips, meaning no word.
Rest your head on the pillow softer than silk, among these little
enchantments, and drink
The forgetfulness tea.
I am Evening: He only pretended to be.

THE BRAIN'S DISSECTION

The brain's dissection,
         after the ritual hanging up by the heels
of the mobbed Mussolini,

Disclosed no lesion peculiar to Roman tyrants
but only the ordinary scar of a small man's hunger for glory.

The crossbow at Agincourt began the decline of the individual
     honor.
The cumbersome knights crawled out of their shells
     like beetles
showing soft bellies,
         the comedy of Quixote de la Mancha.

The smell of the coming years is an odor of
     close-packed bodies,
         the sound is shuffling.
            The leader's no longer the brilliantly separate man,
         the gifted, the visionary,
but the man most like all the others . . .

         Such was *Il Duce*.
         No beggar that crouched upon the sunny steps
            called Spanish
was superior to him nor lesser than him,

         And we, Italia,
the photographers of your ruins and moralists of your ruin,
         what fortune had we that was more than geographic,
         what virtue have we that is more than fortuitous?

Perhaps we have wanted only a yellow moth in an orchard,
     or a girl's mouth, or a boy's,
but the scar of that want in our still private brain-tissue
is neither smaller nor larger than his, exposed,
     that craved empire . . .

     Take it, sun of Italia,
recapture it as your own, and be not ashamed nor proud of it.
Gods passed this way, in this way humanity passes . . .

CREPE-DE-CHINE

When she gives a "psychic reading,"
which isn't likely to be more than once — at the most twice —
    a day,
a set of Oriental glass chimes
        suspended from the ceiling of her
        tackily exotic little "parlor,"
announces that a client has entered.

She calls out hoarsely "Un moment"
        but keeps the customer waiting two or three minutes
before she emerges from her shadowy living-quarters
    with an air of
indifference and fatigue.

        Invariably she is dressed,
        or you might say costumed,
in lavender or rose-colored crepe-de-chine
        shadowy as the room from which she emerges,
and this crumpled apparel is not redeemed
        by her string of dimly opalescent beads.

Usually she will condescend to say "Bonjour" to the client,
        almost as if she were expelling
        her last breath,
and after this ominous greeting she will mumble
    something unintelligible.
      "What?"
      "Nothing. Sit down."

She will then have, or affect to have, a little attack
        of asthma.
            "The dampness of these old houses," she will mutter.
And yet, despite all this atmosphere of fakery,
        the reading will be honest, sometimes distressingly so.

            "I am afraid that you have waited too long to consult
a competent physician."
            "Your idea that you are loved is altogether mistaken."
            "Your employment, I mean the business in which
                you're engaged,
is in so precarious a state that I can only advise you
        to give it up or liquidate it,
and retire to an inexpensive foreign place, perhaps
        some unfashionable
            town in Mexico.
                    Of course I am sorry
to give you this information, but the truth is something
        for which there is no substitute."

When the unnerved client has paid her the variable fee
        and returned
            to the more clement weather of the street
            The Crepe-de-chine,
                    as she is called in "The Quarter,"
must drink a bit of Metaxas
to assuage her true distress, her headache, and
        her exhaustion . . .

LES ETOILES D'UN CIRQUE

For Ingmar Bergman

The stars of a strange circus,
artists on the trapeze,
have taken unusual chances.

All but the elephant have told them
Danger, danger!
They shrug contemptuously.
One of them says
"Our way has always been danger,
and the season is poor."

True enough.
The circus has played in only one
important city
the fiery city of Karl.
Attendance? Disappointing.
It was there, in Karl,
That they discarded the nets
and worked at the top of the tent.

How can they place so little value on their lives
and the continuing life of the circus?
The woman who appears to be headless
in the small, unimpressive sideshow
has sat down, without invitation,
to have coffee with them a while before the performance.
"Tell me why you have discarded the nets
and are working at the top of the tent?"

The two men shrug at her question.
She is persistent.
At last one of them speaks
"The lion died."
"What was the lion," she says, "but a mangy
toothless old cat. The lion? No, not the lion.
The death of the lion's not the reason."

They finish their coffee quickly.

The next stop is Craag.
Ice on the carriage windows, and the road
all but impassable. During
the journey
the clown
raved at the stars of the circus.
"The nets, the nets, don't you know
you'll fall to your deaths without them?"
Answer?
"We're doing what has to be done
in a season too poor for placards."

They fell together like birds descending at Raak.

The circus fell with them, of course.

Performers like apparitions
climbed steep hills
in scattered directions.

The tense of the story has changed.
Now it is *did*, now it is *was*.

The bearded lady (a fake) wrote the woman
who could appear to be headless
"Intentional? Yes. You are right.
They spread their arms like wings
as they plunged from the highest swing
with only space to hold them."

Neither of these wandering apparitions
Knew, or admitted she knew,
that there could have been a reason
beside the poor season
and the death of the old lion.

THE WINE-DRINKERS

The wine-drinkers sit on the porte cochère in the sun.
Their lack of success in love has made them torpid.
They move their fans with a motion that stirs no feather,
the glare of the sun has darkened their complexions.

Let us commend them on their conversations.
One says "oh" and the other says "indeed."

The afternoon must be prolonged forever, because the night
will be impossible for them.
They know that the bright and very delicate needles
inserted beneath the surfaces of their skins
will work after dark — at present are drugged, are dormant.

Nobody dares to make any sudden disturbance.

One says "no," the other one murmurs "why?"
The cousins pause: tumescent.
What do they dream of? Murder?
They dream of lust and they long for violent action
but none occurs.

Their quarrels perpetually die from a lack of momentum
The light is empty: the sun forestalls reflection.

A DAYBREAK THOUGHT FOR MARIA

At daybreak thought
I may die
no reason not
nor reason why

Yet still live
moments through
sky now turning
lighter blue

City woke
as if God spoke
"Cities wake
at daybreak."

Daybreak makes
living wake
and tired move
more to prove

"I live still
ten stories high,
with it moving
still am I"

As if God thought
"Let him go
through at least
one daybreak more."

A LITURGY OF ROSES

I

This is for you for whom bloom certainly roses
This is for you whose reticent temper it is to renounce
the want of all things more effete than rooms full of ferns
without blooms, as bell-shaped conservatories, for whom
a subaqueous green gloom is sufficient without those roses

And yet who have everywhere in their secretive dwellings
beds which are ingeniously disguised as less suggestive
pieces of furniture, such as sofas whose backs collapse into beds
at the touch of a button, oh, and those
suspiciously handsome and languidly moving domestics
are not surreptitious enough to cover up their slow going

to rooms curved as wombs

The warmth of which hums as a transmitter of current
every few hours announcing: Now, yes, now,
now is the moment, yes, now,
A power that draws the light back into its source until you
        let go
and all of those doors floating open on those who have roses
going to those who have roses, in chambers which those
        without roses
possess no license to enter.

II

But I am not sure that I have learned how to let go

Of not particularly caring enough to sicken the heart,
that comfort that should not fail to suffice until later,
oh, considerably later, while moving through rooms
that are lucky with sun until later, the comfort of much later,

While moving through rooms of multiple purposes
and concealed appurtenances
to the heart of abundance from which flow eternally roses,

Roses, all roses, the immense impartiality of all God
and all roses,
orifice emptying, never emptied of roses.

Because you are tolerant only of those who have roses,
Your eyes including the roses of others in bouquets of your own
and saying, These roses, all roses, my roses,
though still in the arms of those who came bearing roses.

And by the same token confessing: My tongue, my tongue,
not your body,
my body, my body, not yours,
while murmuring You, while continually murmuring
You, you, you, which is translated to I
no matter how murmured to whom.

III

Or getting up in the morning and going by plan or caprice
To cut your sweet love's body, mutilating more and more
demoniacally her body, increasing her wounds
and their hemorrhage much faster than she in her running
is rapid enough to stanch them,

And shortly thereafter,
recognizing the need of expedient concealment,

Dragging her purified body into the bathroom and
     dismembering
her purified body in the bathtub, yes, dismembering
carefully, with skill, her purified body
and depositing parts of it

Into those three salty branches that water the Autumn
     rose island

And if you inquire of your love if the water is salty,
your love will reply, It is salty, yes, it is salty.

Are all roses salty? Not altogether but often.

IV

But I am not sure that I have learned how to let go

Of not particularly caring enough to make the heart sick
of anything but those roses,
those white-hot doctors who cauterize our wounds
with irons soft as roses.
All roses, the immense impartiality of all God and all roses,

Announcing, Yes, now as before, yes, now is the moment,
A power that draws the light back into its source,
until you let go and all of those doors floating open
on those who have roses going to those who have roses
in chambers which those without roses have no license to enter.

And it is announced, Yes, now as before, now is the moment,
yes, now

As it was in the vagina, yes, now, as it was in the testicles
and the prostate, as it was in the sperm and the ova,
and as it ever shall be, world without end till we end.

MISS PUMA, MISS WHO?

Miss Puma was popular barely,
you know how such things can be:
in fact, to face matters squarely,
the creep of the forest was she.

She was a continual menace,
a silk hand in the iron glove,
and though she fucked what she could,
there was no discussion of love.

She fucked and would eat what she fucked,
á la Sebastian, you know,
but thus far had met no come-uppance,
no running up street *quid pro quo*.

Suffit and finit introduction
and cut straight to story now.
Miss Puma had overextended
her hand and let me now tell you just how.

There came a night of moon full
and Miss Puma was on the prowl,
creeping at first in silence
then suddenly raising this howl.

"The plentitude of the moon
I find ostentatiously bright.
And off I shall go to the river
And bathe in the shade of the night."

This outcry was somehow disturbing,
her woodland neighbors took fright
and only Miss Monkey remained,
disdaining to join them in flight.

Miss Puma addressed Miss Monkey:
"Many have gone, let them go!
Two swingers are always sufficient
to put on a lively show."

"So come," she said, "to the river
without a moment's delay.
We will go by the underground spring
which is much the amusingest way."

But Miss Monkey was nobody's fool.
She guessed this amusingest way
was the one that just one would emerge from,
but cried back, "Okay, lead the way!"

So they started off for the river
by the subterranean way
that Miss Puma declared so amusing,
Miss Puma leading the way.

The first to arrive was Miss Monkey,
Miss Puma had been delayed,
and the protracted delay of Miss Puma
has gone into late the next day.

"Where, oh, where is Miss Puma?"
Miss Monkey is asked by her friends.
As she bathes in the shade of the river
"Miss *Who?*" is all she will say . . . .

A MENDICANT ORDER

In the bush country of Jamaica
there is a sort of semireligious sect that,
(spelt phonetically, maybe even correctly)
is known as *The Rastrofarians*.

It is a mendicant order and a wandering order
whose members come out of the bush in a stumbling manner
not quite as if they were drunk, perhaps
more as if they were stunned
and none of them seem to be young,
none of them impress me as having ever been young
nor, for that matter, does the question of young or old
seem to be relevant to them.

The men have beards untrimmed and shoulder-length hair
which they seem to have greased with a rust-colored substance.
The women: no beards: otherwise no difference in appearance.
They wander and beg, beg and wander,
drink nothing out of a bottle but I am told that they smoke
something that sounds like ganjah
and just beg and wander, wander and beg, never work.

·　　·　　·

"No good," the driver said of them. We asked "Why?"
He said, indifferently, "Look at them. What are they
　　good for?"
And no immediate answer occurred to me as we passed them:
none then, but later I thought of them, and I thought:

"These people are so used to taking *No* for the answer,
taking it over and over again without protest,
that their mendicancy is absolved of anything shameful,
in fact there's something noble about it, an article of faith
that's pure in belief and in practice."
Then I felt a quiet shame, a feeling that these people,
the Rastrofarians, had offered us a blessing as they stumbled
out of the bush onto the mountain road, that their hands
had been extended not to ask but to give,
and that we had lacked the grace to see and accept their
        blessing.

CINDER HILL

A Narrative Poem

I

Halfway up the Cinder Hill
back of Jamison's stave-mill

was the cottage of Mathilda
who collected pocket silver

from field-hands and stave-mill workers,
grocers' clerks and soda-jerkers,

anyone with half a dollar
and no brighter star to follow.

II

She was neither young nor old,
her hair was red, six teeth were gold

Her frame was large, her bosom very
nearly shamed the local dairy —

Though no beauty, it is true,
Mathilda knew a trick or two

That could give a new sensation
to our oldest recreation.

III

She maintained her social station
for about a generation,

waxed in glory and in wealth
without apparent loss of health.

Then all at once, and God knows why,
Mathilda kissed the boys good-by,

Drew the curtains, latched the door
And gave up practice as a whore.

IV

For a while the town was rife
with rumors of her cloistered life.

was she crippled, was she blind,
had Mathilda lost her mind?

For six years nobody saw her,
the ice man was her only caller

And even he was quite unable
to distinguish fact from fable.

V

So for six years she remained
in retirement unexplained —

Then, for no apparent reason
but that it was budding season,

old Mathilda reappeared,
like the sun when clouds have cleared,

She descended into town
And bought the boys drinks all around.

VI

She was lively, she was loud
as a brass band in a crowd —

Taught a brand new stand of cotton
things their daddies had forgotten —

seemed just like the old Mathilda —
but the effort must have killed her.

Ice man found her one day later
cold as the refrigerator.

VII

Soon Mathilda's former "trade"
came with shovel, came with spade

Came with pick and came with hoe
in the half moon's tender glow —

Dug the earth up all around,
turned up every inch of ground,

It being rumored that Mathilda
had interred her shameful silver

Somewhere in the cinder hill
back of Jamison's stave-mill.

YOU AND I

Who are you?
A surface warm to my fingers,
a solid form, an occupant of space,
a makeshift kind of enjoyment,
a pitiless being who runs away like water,
something left unfinished, out of inferior matter,

Something God thought of.
Nothing, sometimes everything,
something I cannot believe in,
a foolish argument, you, yourself, not I,
an enemy of mine. My lover.

Who am I?
A wounded man, badly bandaged,
a monster among angels or angel among monsters,
a box of questions shaken up and scattered on the floor,

A foot on the stairs, a voice on a wire,
a busy collection of thumbs that imitate fingers,
an enemy of yours. Your lover.

STONES ARE THROWN

I

by an immense Black Man in the circular meadows of heaven.
                    and occasionally we wonder:
Is he alone or can it be that he's attended by subordinate beings
                who do not dare to suggest
that He might limit these acts of an apparent caprice?
                Under thunder the young
of the globe which we still inhabit despite such continual
    hazard
            observe their rituals of the entrance accepted
                and made flesh
and so for a time are enraptured beyond the brutal logistics
          of being and not being which
               cannot become being.

              Stones are thrown
and their impact disastrously known by the aged and diseased
who must present themselves soon at the gate
       of the mineral kingdom.

II

Delirious at daybreak
the young may often know only cataracts of clear water
and so we gasp
since we have sometime clasped
the earliness of their running which was not always away.
Today perhaps
the huge Black Man may cast into space beyond space,
the indefinable void,
a diadem of stars indifferently as a handful of debris,
and light-years after may laugh at the sound which
is echoed back
to his vast circular meadows,
the very slight silvery tinkle of decorous laughter reflecting
an incident which is long past.

THE HARP OF WALES

They do not know through the blood of what witchlike women
the instrument passed unwillingly into their hands
but in it is mist ever clearing and women that keen
among scattered nets at the wet gray edge of the sands.

They cannot guess how the wild harp of Wales came to them,
this ancient of shells in the troubled cleft of their hands,
but schooling was not necessary to master its touch
and the moving of light spells through its transparent strands.

Early they learned of it, often before they were grown,
and forebodings, their own and older, could draw
    from its strings
the moan of those witchlike women who fashioned in Wales
a harp made for keening the deaths of the wild gray kings.

Immutable is the shell, but not the touch,
and possibly now it has an accustomed ring
and the wonder dispelled a degree, but still for a time
it is sorrow not only their own that compels them to sing.

And still for a time they will stay with a sorrow to sing,
with instinct of rules too deep in their blood to forget,
for the wild harp of Wales is enduring among them and cries,
O stay for a time, Thou Stranger, turn not away yet!

THE DIVING BELL

I want to go under the sea in a diving-bell
and return to the surface with ominous wonders to tell.
I want to be able to say:
      "The base is unstable, it's probably unable
      to weather much weather,
being all hung together by a couple of blond hairs caught
in a fine-toothed comb."

I want to be able to say through a P.A. system,
authority giving a sonorous tone to the vowels,
      "I'm speaking from Neptune's bowels.
      The sea's floor is nacreous, filmy
with milk in the wind, the light of an overcast morning."

I want to give warning:
      "The pediment of our land is a lady's comb,
      the basement is moored to the dome
by a pair of blond hairs caught in a delicate
tortoise-shell comb."

I think it is safer to roam
      than to stay in a mortgaged home
        And so —

I want to go under the sea in a bubble of glass
containing a sofa upholstered in green corduroy
and a girl for practical purposes and a boy
      well-versed in the classics.

I want to be first to go down there where action is slow
　　　but thought is surprisingly quick.
　　　It's only a dare-devil's trick,
　　　the length of a burning wick
　　　between tu-whit and tu-who!

　　　Oh, it's pretty and blue
but not at all to be trusted. No matter how deep you go
there's not very much below
　　　the deceptive shimmer and glow
　　　which is all for show
of sunken galleons encrusted with barnacles and doubloons,
an undersea tango palace with instant come and
　　　go moons . . .

HIS MANNER OF RETURNING

It occurs at a time of stillness when you're alone and
    there's that
diffusion of light going into shadow slowly.
       Tall-fenced garden, tropically planted,
    the sun
dropping under palms and sea-grape trees
       between your compound
and the property of the elderly recluse, just before,
    homecoming,
he turns on the lamp's clouded pearl behind his kitchen
    shutters . . .

These being the fore-planned conditions, he is, in a way,
    a visitor
who is invited.
       Then? He appears, a very clear apparition.
Of what was familiar about him there remains a great deal,
    such as
that pride of bearing that makes him seem tall
and his moving about the place in a way that declares it
    his own.

Changes have taken place since he left but they seem not to
    surprise him
and you begin to feel a bit foolish, conducting him about
as you would Garden Ladies on their visiting day in the Spring.

You point out to him the spacious fish pool beneath the outside
staircase, and its witless denizens, the red mollies,
    the pink ones,
the ones that are opalescent.
        He seems not to care for them and, suddenly,
            neither do you.

Then you point out to him the new gazebo in the front
        rose garden,
a lacy white summer confection of a thing that might have
        been meant
for Mme. Arcadina to rustle into at dusk
        (voice clear as a bell ringing vespers)
and for her companion-playwright-lover, Trigorin,
        to look past the fading theatre of her face
at the clear youth of Nina, the sea gull that he'll shoot down,
without intention . . .

To your visitor, pointing at the gazebo, you announce:
"This is the Jane Bowles summerhouse."
And you go on compounding sentiment with sentiment,
        saying
"It's octagonal, you see, eight-sided like all questions are
that many-sided, at least. And on each of its eight sides there
is a brass plate engraved with the name of someone whom
        I've loved.
Here's yours, you see, between the rose vines that are
        beginning
to climb."

Then his detachment gives place
to that old withering way of putting down the Bavarian
      burgher
      in you.
You hear his whispering dryly:
      "Loved? You?"

And so you fall silent beside him, an outcry rising in you
      but held
between throat and tongue, one tasteless indiscretion, this cry
that you will not commit.

    Then?
Something sounds or moves, to the right or left,
and you turn, startled, that way for only a moment.
But the moment's enough, for he only needed that moment
      of inattention
to his presence for him to elude again,
those vulgarities of the living which aren't and never were his
but which you have tried once more to impose on his
      apparition
as if you didn't know that apparitions require a delicacy
      of approach
which isn't your style at all.

Well, now that it's finished, the ceremonial visit,
don't you feel somehow relieved? With the light and shadow
resuming the usual and comfortable order of their retreat
      into nightfall?

All nearly all dark now except for the kitchen lamp of
     the recluse,
back of his kitchen shutters, open a little,
and gently, now, his noiseless hand extended to draw
     them shut?

A gesture of conclusion that's necessary . . .

NIGHT VISIT

It was winter and late at night, an hour or two before the first
gray concession to morning.

                For several weeks
I had been living alone, not answering the telephone
      which had
now grown tired of ringing.
            I had no plans, and was almost comforted somewhat
         by the absence of any.
(What are the plans of a stupefied being?)

On the very few occasions when I had compelled myself
        to go out
I had been tortured by an inability to speak much more than
        an apology
for not speaking.
          In such a condition it is possible to be intolerably lonely
whether you know it or not.

         There was, in the downstairs hall of the highrise
            apartment building
      an electric device that permitted you, if you wished,
to communicate with someone calling you from the guarded
      entrance.
         That late night
it sounded repeatedly and with the irregularity of a failing
      heartbeat.
And I, who had not slept but was stupefied to the point of
        scarcely knowing what I was doing if I did anything,
staggered out of bed at last to answer the call.

"Who is it?"

"Helen."

(A girl who had abruptly disappeared from my life and the lives of everyone I knew who had known her — completely as if she had never existed.)

"Helen?"

"Yes, Helen."

"Helen, I'm pushing the buzzer. Come on up to Apartment C on the twenty-eighth floor."

I met an apparition, and so did she.
She was lovely as ever and even more fragile than ever and
     her eyes
were blind-looking.

I found myself able to think and speak a little.

"What have you been doing lately, Helen?"

Indifferently she said: "When you take pills around
          the clock
what you do is try to get money to pay the drugstore."

Neither of us seemed to care, or to be aware,
that there were such unnatural stretches of silence between
these few things we said.

"Do you know, you must know, about the death of
          my friend?"

"Yes, I know, and I wished that it had been you. Will
you give me cab fare to Olympic, New Jersey?"

I said that I would.

"What pills have you got here?"

I looked more closely at her blind-looking eyes and said that I
    could give her a couple of Milltowns.

    "Big deal. Forget it."

It was like being in a room with a moth that could talk.
    "Helen, you've gotten too thin."
    "Yes, well, I suppose so. Someone I didn't know
came up to me in a bar and said, 'Young lady, you're
    killing yourself.' "
    It was honestly and indifferently reported . . .

A visit late at night, quiet voices, and good-bys that would
    doubtless be final.

ONE AND TWO

One: (*slowly and gravely*)
> You sit in this hard bright room with your abstract
>> pictures.
> All your confessions are only made to yourself.
> You never conveniently drop your private journal on
>> the stairs.
> How can another person ever get near you?

Two: (*dully*)
> Why should another person want to get near me?
One: (*looking out of the window*)
> Loneliness.
Two:
> Whose? Not mine.

One: (*with a touch of asperity*)
> You sit in this hard bright room with your abstract
>> pictures.
> Try to tell me that you are satisfied with it!
Two: (*flicking an ash from a Russian cigarette*)
> One of my earliest discoveries about life was the usual
> lack of very much satisfaction among the living.

One:
> But surely you could improve your situation.
Two: (*lifting an eyebrow*)
> How? By including you in it?
One: (*flushing slightly*)
> Possibly. — Yes, — why not?

Two:

>Because you're childish, darling.
>
>You don't seem to understand how anyone, having to choose between something and nothing, might choose nothing because he wanted something.
>
>Oh, by the way — if you happen to go in town, you might drop by the commissary for me.

One: (*grinning somewhat bitterly*)

>What do you want?

Two:

>A roll of toilet paper, a box of matches, a quart of kerosene for the kitchen burner.

One:

>Yes. — Good-by.

TWO POEMS FROM
THE TWO-CHARACTER PLAY

I

Fear is a monster vast as night —
And shadow casting as the sun.
It is quicksilver, quick as light —
It slides beneath the down-pressed thumb.
Last night we locked it from the house.
But caught a glimpse of it today.
In a corner, like a mouse.
Gnawing all four walls away.

II

Old beaux and faded ladies play
    on Cypress Boulevard
games of talkative croquet
    as shadows cross the yard

Or underneath green awnings pause
    in lavender and white
until the cats of jeweled claws
    glide down the walls of night

Softly to crouch with bated breath
    and glare at all below,
their malice on each upturned face
    descending cool as snow.

THE LADY WITH NO ONE AT ALL

Milady has picked up a whisper of lilac chiffon
and thrown it about her shoulders in the
      afternoon-dimming hall.
It is an hour when desolation is most inclined to assail her.
"I am feeling somewhat older, you know,
although I don't really look it, I don't think I look it at all.
Of course the skin loses some tone, actually more in most cases,
but a fine bone-structure always remains unimpaired."

She is turning before a cracked pier-glass in the hall,
turning and turning slowly and speaking to no one at all.

"To me the days seem longer in the fall.
It's restlessness, I suppose, or the after effect of fever."

A sweep of fantasy, then:
"Oh, how I'd love to be lifted in a silk-curtained palanquin,
how lovely to be lifted in a silk-curtained palanquin!
— or carried South on the wind . . ."

(His silence continues: this recent remote attitude
has persisted disturbingly long:
plans of travel abandoned: so much inaction is wrong.)

"Do you know what I would prefer to backgammon?" she calls,
"I'd much more enjoy a bit of fair weather boating
about on the pond, wouldn't you?
Before the sun goes, let's do row about on the pond!"

Again there's a pause which is silence.
                              Milady interprets it, though,
as the soft-spoken assent of him who is no one at all.

"Well, do hurry, the sun won't last long, you know,
and it's exasperating to be kept continually waiting,
I will go onto the lawn."

And so now Milady has wandered onto the gently
        down-sloping lawn
from which the late afternoon sun
has not yet completely withdrawn.

"I'm feeling a bit light-headed, my fever hasn't quite gone."
But she goes with the slope of the lawn,
she lifts the hem of her white linen skirt,
steps out of her slippers and, bare-footed, descends
unsteadily to the pond.

"Old father of ten generations!"
        (She is addressing the drake
at the marshy edge of the pond which is nearly large as a lake.)
"Ten faithless generations, all of them flown
at the first warning of Fall: but you'll not fly
nor would I."

She has now stumbled into the boat,
she has disengaged it from its loose-knotted rope
and it is adrift on the pond.

"Oh, no, please don't!" she cries out,
mistaking a pain in her groin
for fingers remembered as given to intimate probing.

Then closing her eyes for a moment, she consoles him with
"Later, please wait until a bit later . . ."

"Do you know how very much and constantly
I have loved you?" she whispers to him,
leaning to brush with her lips the lips of no one at all.

Anticipating the delayed season of Fall,
a chill wind has twisted her whisper of lilac chiffon,
penetrating her fever for a moment which now has
     already gone
a long way over the lawn's
shadowy slope to the pond, nearly as large as a lake.

At its marshy verge the drake's
dark eyes are turning opaque,
But not the eyes of Milady who is serenely still boating,
she is still floating and floating,
she is late-afternoon boating with him who is no one at all.

I have sensed that somewhere about the premises which
    I inhabit,
        probably in its storm-wracked attic,
There lives a dark and cunning old creature
    whom I know as the spider,
        obsessively industrious, adaptable to whatever
conditions
have thus far assailed him in his secluded corner.
        And so I think of him as the loom of my heart.
        This creature receives assignments that shake him,
            that make his ancient web tremble,
but he rarely, if ever, declines them,
    knowing what's left of his craft,
        and what's still expected of it.

        However, lately,
via Special Delivery, he has been sent what is more an edict,
        a command to perform an all but impossible task
to somehow weave together a pair of enormous and thoroughly
    incompatible
        abstractions
called *time* and *peace*.
        Christ, how it stuns him,
        how it trembles the web! Still, he's immobilized
for a moment only: then habit is re-established and he
    undertakes it . . .

       •   •   •

About this creature, the spider: he's nameless though
                    most familiar,
performs in solitude which is soundless and lightless
                    and little as that may be, no more can be disclosed.
                    time and *peace*,
weave them somehow together, there's his latest and
        probably last
undertaking and he is going about it as best he is able.

•   •   •

            And now, however abruptly, let me descend
to the objective, hoping it won't be repellent to sensibilities
of a more delicate nature than the old spider's.
            Well, it is three A.M.
after an hour's sleep and a blond youth who declined to
        stay with me.
            Wolf's hour of night is not well-spent alone.

Delayed or premature contractions of a damaged heart-valve
                    accent the dark outside
windows shut on the clamor of the collectors of the debris,
brute anguish of trucks clearning the street by suction.
            Nevertheless there is this bit of comfort:
in my hands' curved remembrance there remains indelibly
the unclothed flesh of the youth who refused to stay longer,
                    and I could settle for less,
                    God knows if not unknowing.

As for the spider, I hear his loom shuttling away in
that much-weathered top story. He may glance up,
rather
quickly and inscrutably dimly
from the possibly impossible
task imposed on him.
            My guess is that
the incalculably ancient creature
has grudgingly accepted the fact that this last work ordered
        of him
is not only appropriate, now, but probably well-intended.
            Otherwise, would he continue? Till confronted
with the last, unchangeable red STOP sign?

THE ICE-BLUE WIND

Being expert on the zither
he gave concerts twice a winter

And to these occasions twain
some would come unless it rained

Swifly did their number thin
as he played *The Ice-Blue Wind*.

No cries of Bravo nor encore
But, Oh, he dreamed, they long for more!

So he'd play it once again
and again and still again.

His fingers knew The Ice-Blue Wind
that single score and nothing more.

But what of that? It did suffice
to close him in a wall of ice,

Tinged with distance, always blue,
which somehow warmed him through and through.

Long, long after all had gone,
and in the hall crept winter dawn,

He would strike a final string,
take a bow and proudly shin

Up a column to the roof,
in union with The Absolute.

TURNING OUT THE BEDSIDE LAMP

Turning out the bedside lamp
is an act to whose eventual necessity I surrender
with ever increasing reluctance,

delaying it by reading beyond my limit
of concentration on an article or a story,
taking an extra wine-glass of Dry Sack sherry, placing
the sleeping capsule where I can locate it easily
in the dark, should the preliminary tablet of Valium
      not suffice,

Because, you see, at sixty-five
abdicating your consciousness to sleep
involves, usually, a touch of nervous apprehension
that it may not ever revive. However

I sometimes suspect that there's
a certain luxury submerged in this: a touch of
concealed fascination in the surrender as well . . .

TANGIER: THE SPEECHLESS SUMMER

I

I hear it is clear today but I don't want to see it.
How can I keep it away?
At noon the drum of the sun is, yes, already begun,
and the time of an appointment
cannot be stayed, although the imminence of it
is drawing much tighter the tight muscles of my throat,
this summer's home of my torment.

Punctually at one my friend Paul comes, and we walk through
the Medina.
(Is it thatch-roofed?
Stitches of light seem to kindle the crisp curled gold of
his hair
and his thin-burned face which is always so concentrated.)
Do I talk to him?
Only a few precisely spaced and forced observations of what
I imagine
he must have daily observed and nothing at all of the panic
of which I longed to speak to him.
He says, "Oh, here," and enters a shop, and while he is
bargaining for
purchases I lose myself in a confusion of shoppers, hoping that
he will
ascribe my disappearance to this easily-lost-in confusion . . .

I love Paul, but once he said to me: "I've never had a neurosis."

•   •   •

Last night, oh, yes, last night the rain crept soundlessly down
as if ashamed of its detested recurrence, obsequiously
    respectful
of consulate flags, or simply speechless as I am . . .
In Tangier all non-Mohammedan visitors and residents are
    called Nazarenes
and are polar-ized by white weather that's reminiscent of
    sunlight that's
            never truly existed.
The mythically established ones gather in a conspiratorial
    manner
at elaborate garden dinners and inquire of each other
            is he or he or he "safe,"
a question that seems to be filtered endlessly through an
    echo chamber.
            Does it have a dependable answer?
My guess would be no but my presence here has been brief,
            and with so much night rain . . .

    II

            My young companion, "The Poet."
Fair as Adonis but rational as ten hatters at Alice's tea-party.
        Seems to be succumbing to my iron of silence
        which is so desperately unwillful.
        Can he still, at times, like me?
Can magic still, at times, be the order of our existence?
He can, at times, offer a comforting dimness to rooms
    still lighted
and rooms aren't always lighted.
            Apart from the garden dinners,

to which this attractive companion is actually, of course,
the one that's truly invited
we follow an all but unalterable evening program.
We go to the Zoco Chico for hot mint tea with jiggers
of rum in it.
Will it loosen my tongue? Effectually, not
just enough to say: "Let's go."

Why don't I pretend that a growth on my vocal chords has
made it necessary
to have them at once cut away, say,
in Gilbraltar?
I could have this bit of not much too false information
printed in clear block letters on pieces of cardboard
which I could pass out gravely at all social occasions.

Or go on "H."
Shouldn't everyone go on "H" before they die, and be certain
of their supply?
How pleasant it surely would be
to drift above the tree-tops, invisible, unheard,
unsuspected,
serenely detached from the troublesome matter
of speech,
all panic locked in a closet, yes, elect the cool death.

III

The straits between here and England's Rock are a damp piece
    of water
        that barely acknowledges any day to be clear.
I've often seen them (subjectively) when they were
    the bedsheets
of someone just dead of convulsions.
           And yet last night my talented
              young friend and I
    leaned on a window sill to catch the slow rain
      in a cup —
        the purest water . . .

             •   •   •

Jane, I said to you: "Jane, I can't talk anymore."
and you said to me: "Tennessee, you were never much of
    a talker."
    The long, white beach and the wanderers along it,
    we recognized, silently, its emptiness, much populated.
The Nazarene (mythical) with the elegantly aged
    Rolls-Royce.
        Quote:
    "I wouldn't be caught dead in a Silver Cloud."
    No day is finished but discontinued a while.